That's Terrible!

A Cringeworthy Collection of 1001 Really Bad Jokes

By

Gary Rowley

For Lindsay, Laura and Roly Rowley, best dog in the world, sorely missed x

...So there I was, chuckling away at another rib-tickling text message, when I thought, I could do that. What you are reading now is the result of my efforts, 1001 predominantly original jokes and one-liners, plumbed from the innermost depths and far-out corridors of what, I am assured, is an extremely vivid imagination. All the jokes are good, clean fun, free from profanity, and the perfect pick-me-up, to mention nothing of ideal text message fodder. All you need to do to become immersed in this barrage of off-the-wall buffoonery is find a quiet spot somewhere then slowly turn the page...

Enjoy!

Mobile phones have been around longer than people think. I was watching this film the other day and heard Sir Lancelot ask someone to fetch his charger.

I was considering investing in a Chinese distillery but decided against it. Whiskey business.

I went to the waxworks but legged it when I saw this woman coming towards me, swinging a pair of giant blades. I discovered later it was Madame Two Swords.

Michael Phelps and the Thorpedo: they think they're God's gift to swimming.

I had a go on the Go Compare website. Next thing I knew, I was presenting Strictly Come Dancing.

As an ex-paratrooper, I definitely thought my bill for dental work was a bridge too far.

I had a real bad accident at the saw mill. My other half says we should sue for compensation.

I've just lost my job at the snuff factory. I was sacked for pinching.

A mother, father, brother, sister, aunt, uncle and fourteen cousins all joined forces to change a light bulb. Many hands make light work.

So I said, waiter, this coffee tastes like mud. He said, what do you expect? It was only ground half an hour ago.

I walked into Leeds station and asked the route to Bristol. I said, is it Leeds to Sheffield, then Derby, Birmingham, Cheltenham Spa and Gloucester? He said, it's somewhere along those lines.

Someone said there was a decent turn on at the working men's club. When I got there, it was an Arctic sea bird with a big, yellow beak.

I found my hotel bathroom stuffed with chickens. It was hen-suite.

Boy racers. They're the torque of the town.

I always fancy my chances at the casino. In recent weeks, I've fallen in love with a pack of playing cards and a roulette wheel.

I went to this christening and the church went up in flames. Talk about baptism of fire.

Every time it's nice outside, there's this American pop duo that stand on a street corner, giving money away. It's Sunny and Share.

I asked a bloke in a Winnie the Pooh costume the way to the bus station, and he sent me in completely the wrong direction. I'm sure he did it on purpose, the bear faced liar.

I was walking behind this bloke when an arrow shot from between his knees and took my hat off. He was obviously bow-legged.

I've just seen a bloke in pyjamas, snoring his head off as he ran the hundred metres in 9.7 seconds. I thought, now that's what you call fast asleep.

Everyone thinks I'm playing the part of Santa at the Christmas party. Little do they know, but I've got the perfect get out Claus.

I phoned Mountain Rescue when I got into difficulty in the hiking shop. I said, come and get me. You'll find me on the aisle of Arran.

I attended a shoe repairer's convention the other day. Honestly, it was a right load of cobblers.

My new girlfriend bought chicken, onion, peppers and tortilla rolls for tea. She obviously thinks I'm a faji-eater.

I went for a passport photo and finished up with a picture of some bloke handing his girlfriend a glass of vintage ruby.

McDonald's Drive Thru. It's like talking to a brick wall.

I've just seen a rough-looking policeman on the beat minus handcuffs. I thought, I bet he doesn't take any prisoners.

The new bakery owner has bright red hair. He's a ginger bread man.

I'm worried my mum is money laundering. She's just washed my jeans with twenty quid in the back pocket.

That bloke on Thunderbirds asks a lot of questions, doesn't he? He's a right nosey Parker.

I was guest speaker at the herb association AGM yesterday but hardly anyone turned up. What a waste of thyme.

Bad tempered window cleaners. They always lose their rag.

When I spilled my drink in the cafe, I grabbed a mug off the next table. I soon gave it back, though: it wasn't my cup of tea.

I went in a pub in Nottingham and was shocked to see Robin Hood and his merry men, sitting in a corner, drinking fizzy pop. I thought, ooh look, archers and lemonade.

My pen ran out yesterday. It was last seen crossing the road in the direction of the park.

I arrived home to find burglars making off with my Walt Disney collection. I thought, they're taking the Mickey.

The best way to serve fresh pancakes? Easy peasy, lemon squeezy.

It's just been announced that the PM's scalp is infested with mites from the Downing Street parrot. That's polly-ticks for you.

I used to be an American police car, but I'm not now, wow, wow, wow, wow, wow...

I went in Curry's and asked for Blu-Ray. They put a call out over the tannoy, and this bloke appeared. It said Ray on his shirt, and he was completely blue from head to foot.

The toilet was blocked, so I called out a plumber. He gave it a Lemsip and sent it to bed with a hot water bottle.

This plank of mahogany said, so, you wanna piece of me? It was hard wood.

I saw a violin, racing a viola round the athletics track. They were both as fit as fiddles.

Greenwich Mean Time. It's daylight robbery.

I'm unconvinced about my new job at the pizza parlour. I suppose I'll just have to see how it pans out.

Peter Andre is dating a woman who is always crying and looks like Red Rum. His new single miss teary horse girl is released next week.

I used to be a parrot but I'm not now. I used to be a parrot but I'm not now...

I bumped into Steven Spielberg, lost on his way to the Oscars. No sense of direction.

I said, where's Panavision, Mr Spielberg? He said, never heard of it. I said, you liar. Your last movie was filmed there.

My maths teacher asked me to calculate the number of seconds in a century. I thought, that will be a test of time.

When I was in the army, I was given a platoon of ex-basketball players to whip into shape. Talk about a tall order.

I ran for my life when I stumbled across a tribe of starving cannibals. I thought, they'll have my guts for starters.

Rooney placed the ball in the quadrant and the linesman lit a fag. It was smoker's corner.

All seater stadiums. I can't stand them.

I bought Blackpool Pleasure Beach yesterday. Last week, I bought Alton Towers and the week before that, Lightwater Valley. I got them from the office of fair trading.

My friend bought a pile of old vinyl off Ebay. I said, let's have a Decca.

I said to the wife, nip down the shops and buy corned beef, potatoes, leeks, carrots and onions. And don't make a hash of it.

What did Field Marshall Rommel say to his men just before they got into their tanks? Come on now, lads, get in them tanks.

I was working in this stone quarry near Liverpool when a landslide left me pinned to the floor. I thought, brilliant, now I'm stuck between a rock and a hard place.

I said, waiter, this meat's tough as old boots. He said, what do you expect, you're in Liverpool?

I went in HMV. I said, how much is your cheapest classical music box set? He said, three tenors?

More people were flocking to the funeral than attending the village fair. It was obviously a fete worse than death.

I said, doctor, I keep thinking I'm John McEnroe. He said, you *cannot* be serious!

There's this woman near me who struts around like C-3P0 out of Star Wars. Her name is Ann Droid.

I've just seen Ringo Starr, driving a Herbie car. I thought, ooh look, Volkswagen Beatle.

When I caught the barman stealing beer from my pub, I let him have it. Both empty barrels.

I was walking down the street when kings and queens began falling from the sky. It was raining monarchs.

I saw Tom Thumb yesterday in Wacky Warehouse. I thought, it's time he grew up a bit.

I saw a horse box today. It won on points over ten rounds.

My friend is so down to earth. He crawls everywhere on his stomach.

I went to an exhibition of 18th Century Dutch Impressionists' but left disappointed. Hadn't they heard of Salford Van Hire?

I saw a sign on the motorway saying, free recovery. I thought, free Rick who?

The fishing mad dentist typed into his sat nav: route canal.

I'm holidaying in the Far East this year. Cleethorpes.

I was woken at three in the morning by a bloke in a red coat, cocked hat and ceremonial chain, giving a speech at the foot of my bed. Talk about a night mayor.

I work as a lift engineer. It's not a bad job, but certainly has its share of ups and downs.

My first wife used to eat maths text books. She was very full figured.

I booked in at the Ritz. Imagine my disappointment when I ended up spending the night in a box of salted crackers.

I've just seen a tramp, driving a Bentley. Honestly, it beggars belief.

I was once a prison warden, guarding the Birdman of Alcatraz. I watched him like a hawk.

Mr Burgin from the takeaway is the most obnoxious bloke I've ever come across. Talk about a chip on his shoulder.

It's just been announced that, with regret, the Southend Deckchair Manufacturing Company has now folded.

I went into this plant hire shop. I said, can I rent a yucca till a week on Sunday?

My mate reckons he earns five hundred pounds per week, hosing down pigs at the farm. If you want my opinion, it's complete and utter hogwash.

I saw this van with a sign on the back saying, how's my driving? So I pulled up alongside and shouted, not bad but you need to practise your long puts.

Did you know they've stopped selling Red Bull in Boots? Apparently it leaks out of the lace holes.

I popped into this Spar shop. When I came out, I had two black eyes.

I hear the organisers of the Royal Albert Hall forgot to book an orchestra for last week's concert. I've absolutely no symphony for them.

When I was in the army, I used to eat nothing but ice-cream, lemon meringue and chocolate fudge cake. I was a desserter.

I heard this bush meowing. It must have been a pussy willow.

There was this sign on the motorway which said, queue on slip road. When I got there, it was Q out of James Bond, fixing a rocket launcher to the Aston Martin DB5.

I've just started up a tree felling business. If things take off, I'll soon have branches nationwide.

I used to think I was this big, Egyptian river. Now I'm in denial.

There was a sign in the supermarket saying, manager's special. I wouldn't have gone that far, but I suppose everyone's entitled to their opinion.

I bought a sweatshirt. It was cold, clammy and the stench made me vomit.

My watch is slow. It's hopeless at maths and doesn't even know the capital of France.

I was working in B&Q when this bloke came up and asked if I could show him where to find those horizontal bubble contraptions that brickies used. I said, I'll do my level best.

I discovered a six-foot hole in my garden. Next day, it was ten-foot, and the day after that twenty. I thought, hmmm, I'm going to have to get to the bottom of this...

My name is mud. I've just dropped my passport in a filthy puddle.

I've lost my bank book. If anyone finds it, I can recommend the chapter on Barclays.

My friend is fishing mad. He even bought a house on Avon Close as tribute to his favourite river. Just in case you wondered, I live at 32 Spearmint Rhino Avenue.

When I put the rubbish out, I couldn't help noticing all the black sacks were still intact from the night before. There was obviously a wildcat strike on.

My doctor used to be in the army. It even says so on the practice letterhead. Apparently he was known as General Practitioner.

I went in my favourite restaurant. The waiter said, your steak is cooked to perfection, sir. I said, well done.

He said, you did want steak, didn't you, sir? I said, it would be rare if I didn't.

I saw this bloke on his way out of the RSPB sanctuary with a sick bird under his arm. I said, you can't take that with you, mate. He said, why not? I said, because you can't. It's ill eagle.

I used to be a postman in China, but got fed up of rowing out to sea to deliver all the junk mail.

My dentist had a hand rammed down my throat for ages. I thought, it's about time he got his finger out...

I had a pee on my telephone directory last night: Yellow pages.

A friend of mine collects waterproof, padded jackets. What an anorak.

I took a telephone canvassing call that went: cluck-cluck, cluck-cluck, cluck-cluck. It was someone calling from Hen Power.

My carnivorous friend called. He said, meat me in the butchers.

I watched Dirty Dancing through the window of an in-flight Boeing 707. It was on sky movies.

I saw a bloke in a sombrero, driving up a dead end street. I thought, no way Jose.

Sheep herding. It's a dog's life.

The price of diesel is getting beyond a joke. It cost me two grand yesterday to fill the tank up. Honestly, I rue the day I ever laid eyes upon that army surplus, Russian made T-34.

I've got a little window over my Adam's apple. It's a right pane in the neck.

I can't stand the ringmaster at the circus where I work. I'm sick of jumping through hoops for him.

What do cannibals take for indigestion? Aunt acid.

I drove past a 24 hour garage the other day. I drove past again 24 hours later and, sure enough, it was gone.

Every time I get in my car, it sends me to sleep. It's a VW Bora.

I stopped at a hole in the wall yesterday. It was eight inches by four, and I had it bricked up again in next to no time.

I made a delivery to this American warship. I said to the captain, what on earth do you want three tons of fresh herring, a set of hoops and a balancing ball for? He said, you've heard of the US Navy Seals, haven't you?

I saw one of those witchetty things, having a pint in my local. I thought, ooh look, pub grub.

I bought this paper shop. When it didn't do much, I shut it down and put it out for recycling.

This bloke sneezed, and all the water droplets began swearing and generally acting offensive. Talk about a common cold.

I got that trainee astronaut's job at NASA. I'm absolutely over the moon.

My physics teacher said, what can you tell me about atomic number one? I said, it was released on the Chrysalis label and was a big hit for Blondie in 1981.

I saw this sign on a garage forecourt saying, Max height 11'9". I thought, wow, I bet no one drives off without paying at Max's garage.

Back on the road, I spotted another sign, which said, Max speed 60. I thought, crikey, he's quick off the mark as well.

I've just seen Annie Lennox and Dave Stewart, working down at A&E. Apparently they've reformed as the Eurythmedics.

I was in the pub when this woman picked up a glass of Chardonnay and began howling like a puppy dog. I thought, whey hey, whine by the glass.

There was this bloke streaking round the optician's today. Honestly, he made a right spectacle of himself.

I saw two lumps of iron having a fight. It was obviously scrap metal.

My eyesight is getting worse. When I spotted a sign saying, humps for 200 yards, it never once crossed my mind that I might be in the camel enclosure at Chester Zoo.

I asked this bloke for directions. He said, carry straight on over seven islands. At the eighth island, turn left, then straight across six more islands, before turning right at the seventh island. Straight across nineteen more islands, and then you should see it on the left-hand-side. I got there in the end. In a roundabout kind of way, anyway.

I was visiting the Acropolis when this bloke came up to me and said, Αθήνα είναι πραγματικά όμορφη στο καλοκαίρι. I just ignored him. It was all Greek to me.

I went to the pub and discovered Rupert, Biffo, Paddington and Winnie the Pooh out the back, enjoying a pint of mild. I thought, aye-aye, a bear garden.

I've just seen a hamburger, driving a Lamborghini. I thought, whey hey, fast food.

I took my Mars bar back to the shop because it wouldn't stop chanting rhyming lyrics. I felt such a fool when the shopkeeper explained it was just the Rapper.

This waiter looked me up and down then said, rack of ribs? I said, not really, I've just been cutting back of late.

I must have been on a trunk road tonight because every car I passed was driven by an elephant.

There's this OAP, who stands to attention in the corner of my best mate's living room, dressed like a chicken and making tick-tock-boing noises. It's his grandfather cluck.

I love flying. But it doesn't half make my arms ache.

Butch Cassidy and the Sundance Kid turned up at my house to start work on the new extension. I thought, just what I need: cowboy builders.

I used to be in an elite cavalry unit. Special horses, actually.

I saw a vicar, chasing devils round a running track. He was exercising a few demons.

I've just had my house draught-proofed. This company came round and proved inconclusively: I definitely have a draught.

Me and the bloke who invented reclining chairs: we don't half go back a long way.

I sailed round the world in a bank. Chartered, naturally.

I gatecrashed this party only to find it stuffed with Howitzers in suits and gowns, dancing a waltz. Then I realised: it was a cannon ball.

I assassinated a camel. I bumped it off.

A horrendous thunderstorm erupted in the cafe, fork lightning and pouring rain. Talk about a storm in a teacup.

I've visited football grounds all over the country but never been to Man City. Frankly, I don't fancy visiting anywhere completely devoid of women.

I was at the football match when my palm started crying. It happened straight after the crowd shouted, hand bawl!

I've just been made redundant from my job at the bank. Not that I care. I was going to pack it in, anyway. There was no money in it.

I'm taking time out. My new girlfriend is an alarm clock.

I asked this woman's tibia and fibula out on a date. She said, are you pulling my leg?

I've just seen a hundred men, all with fingers stuck up their noses. It was a picket line.

My son ate nothing but ice-cream for 31 days. Month of sundae's.

There was this fantastic programme on last night about how blue bottles use suction to adhere themselves to vertical surfaces. It was a fly on the wall documentary.

I'm all in favour of corporal punishment. If you ask me, he's the best NCO in the army.

I've just seen a boot boy, devouring fish, chips and mushy peas in under a minute. I thought, crikey, he soon polished that off.

Inflation is really getting out of hand. I've just paid a quid for a penny arrow.

I told my wife her new hairstyle reminded me of a mop. She absolutely wiped the floor with me.

I came across some deadwood on the beach. I put my coat over it.

There was a new moon last night. I know because someone left the tag on it.

I can see the woods from my back window. The Woods are the family next door. At the bottom of their garden is a sewage plant.

I once lived in a house with no electric. It was like living in the dark ages.

Sixteen donkeys have perished in mysterious circumstances. Police fear an ass murderer may be at large.

I used to have an earwig. Well, two in actual fact. They were littlemats of hair, which I used to place over each lobe.

I thought the approaching clamour of pounding music was a ghetto-blaster at first. Then I realised: it was a tranny-van.

Every sheep in the flock lost its voice. Baa none.

I'm on the graveyard shift this week. I'm working nights in a cemetery.

I was watching this kung fu film when the wife arrived home unexpectedly. I thought, what a coincidence: Enter the Dragon.

Thousands of pounds have gone missing from a safe at the ketchup factory. Main suspect is the company accountant...if sauces are to be believed.

This waiter fetched me a glass of smiling pop. I said, what's this? He said, it's your happy Tizer.

I've just seen Norman Schwarzkopf coming out of casualty. It was the general hospital.

Did you know Jar Jar Binks' brother has BO? He's Jar Jar Stinks.

I dropped off 24 cans of beer at the barbecue. The blokes waiting for a haircut were ever so appreciative.

This may sound like pie in the sky...but I'll swear I've just seen a flying Cornish pasty.

I joined a fan club. How cool is that?

A barrel of oil gave me a mouthful. I said, don't be so crude.

I went into HMV. I said, do you have anything by the Beach Boys? The assistant said, I usually have pina colada, but my mate here prefers cold beer.

I thought last night's programme about cheating raisins was excellent. Which is odd, because I'm not usually into currant affairs.

Mulled wine? Not in my house. We just go for it.

I've just seen a chicken, splashing around at the sewage farm. It was poultry in motion.

I went to the seaside and spotted a huge humpback, wearing a crown. It reckon it must have been the prince of whales

Vidiprinter manufacturing: it's a results business.

I was in the Queen's arms last night. She mistook me for a relative of Prince Phillip's and gave me a big hug in the kebab house.

I saw a bus load of saluting soldiers on the M1. I thought, what's going on here? Then I realised: it was major roadworks.

This kid offered to sell me a pair of boots with wheels for seventy-five pence. I said, you're such a cheap skate.

I've started work at the casino. It's not my idea of fun, but I suppose I'm just going to have to learn to deal with it.

I once worked in a family-run florists'. Grandma and Granddad were great. So was Dad. My main gripe was with Chris an' the Mum.

My wife always buys the first thing she sees, and usually the most expensive. She's my nearest and dearest.

I've just had the traffic news on. The presenter was a 51 plate Ford Focus.

I'm scared of sun, wind, rain, hail, sleet, snow, mist, fog, thunder and lightning. I live in a climate of fear.

Tornadoes. They put the wind up me.

I saw this policeman, dressed as a Messerschmitt 109. He was in plane clothes.

Two chavs window-shopping outside Carphone Warehouse. One said, that's the one I'd get. Cyclops said, you talking about me?

I was driving to work this morning and noticed everyone had a mobile phone glued to their ear. Then I realised: I was on the ring road.

It's been on Spanish news that bathers caught relieving themselves in the Mediterranean will be now be prosecuted. Let's hope that appeases the pee sea brigade.

I couldn't believe it when water began pouring from my new iPhone. I thought, this has been tapped.

We get a ghost in our house every Christmas. It's the festive spirit.

I watched Lord of the Rings on DVD last night. Brilliant film. I might give WH Smith a call and see if the book is out yet.

When the weatherman said it was going to be frosty, the last thing I expected to find was a covering of sugar-coated cornflakes.

I saw a sign saying, ready mix concrete. I thought, I wonder if anyone's thought of telling Mick?

I got out of the car and fell down. No wonder. I was on a slip road.

A security guard has been charged with theft following the disappearance of umpteen pallets of washing up liquid from a distribution centre. He'd always maintained masked thieves were responsible. But a police spokesman said they knew from the start this was a Fairy story.

I went to church on Sunday and the vicar was dressed in a Scooby Doo outfit. It was a blessing in disguise.

This morning I will sell ten packets. This afternoon I will sell nineteen. Tomorrow I will sell thirty, and the day after that thirty more. This was the Werther forecast, brought to you courtesy of Patel's convenience store, Birmingham.

I went to this restaurant and there was a sign outside saying, no fly tipping. When I got inside, all the waiters were blue bottles.

Classic sixties film The Italian Job: they're making a new mini-series.

I've started up a company manufacturing trifles. Look out for my ad' in jello pages.

I asked my mate how many cigarettes he smoked per day. Forty? Fifty? He said, and some. I said, you what? Have you looked in the mirror recently?

So I said, if every cigarette takes three minutes off your life, how come you didn't you pop your clogs in 1776?

I was in New Orleans and saw a street car go past, filled with spuds. It was a street car named Desiree.

New Orleans. Rumour has it there's a house there.

I booked a trip to Lourdes but got on the wrong bus. England finished the day on 489 for 6.

Every night, a horse gallops past my window. I'm sick of these recurrent night mares.

Is Anti-Semitism the England football team's inability to progress beyond the quarter finals of a major tournament?

We have a three-bedroomed semi-detached staying in the spare room for a couple of weeks. It's a guest house.

I had a Big Mac for dinner. I'm extremely partial to XXXL raincoats.

I went to see the new doctor. He had a skinhead haircut and was wearing boots and braces. It was Doc Martin.

The cashier commented how tired I looked after walking eighteen miles to visit the Swedish self-assembly furniture shop where she worked. I said, well it does say hike here, doesn't it?

Poetry: I can't say I'm averse to it.

I was on HMS Bounty when this sailor spilled rum down Captain Bligh's uniform. I thought, there's going to be a back lash over this.

I saw lasagne on a skateboard, fish and chips on a bike, and a Big Mac meal driving a Vauxhall Corsa. I thought, ooh look, meals on wheels.

There was this cat, waiting for a prescription on Christmas Eve. It was puss in Boots.

I went to Liverpool and couldn't believe how many people were on their way to see some woman who goes by the name of Ann Field.

I took my girlfriend to see Free Willy. Half way through, I popped to the toilet and...Anyway, it was a really good film.

Walking past the surgical wing of the local hospital, I spotted a sign saying, CCTV in operation. I thought, cripes, I hope it's not serious.

I visited Buckingham Palace and noticed lots of activity in the kitchen area. They were changing the lard.

I went to the Tower of London next and saw a dozen Beefeaters, munching on salad sandwiches.

Big Ben. You wouldn't want to mess with him.

My mother-in-law is adamant our new-born baby has my eyes. I said, if that's the case, can you please explain how they're still in my head?

I bought a new toilet from B&Q. Nothing fancy, just bog standard.

I was doing my homework when water suddenly started spurting everywhere. It's the last time you'll catch me using a blooming fountain pen.

My best friend's a real wide boy. He has a 102 inch waist.

I was in Humberside's new Disney Store when a fight broke out over a Jungle Book DVD. Honestly, it was a right Hull-a-Baloo.

That job at the kitchen worktop factory, it looks like I've got it. Touch Formica.

I went to the test match, and the umpire was covered in feathers and eating worms. It must have been Dickie Bird.

I've been reading a book about the history of bananas. It's called the Chronicles of Nana.

A Hammerhead shark accosted a pasty-faced squid, dragging it half way across the ocean, before handing it over to a vicious looking Great White. There you go, Jaws, it said, there's that sick squid I owe you.

I was passing the magistrates court and noticed a series of letters, strung between two lampposts, spelling out the words 'guilty as charged, two years at Her Majesty's pleasure'. It was a suspended sentence.

Apparently burglars ran amok in the litter bin factory last night. They absolutely trashed the place.

I was in the VW garage when this bloke said, Passat. So I handed him a trilby off the next table.

The light went out. It didn't say where...

I was outside the pub yesterday, downing a swift one, when the manager of the DSS appeared. He said, don't you get tired of lounging around all day? I thought, I suppose I do. So I caught the bus home and went straight to bed.

I was in the chippie, listening the obese assistant, regaling customers upon the meaning of life. I thought, she's a deep fat fryer.

That film's on again this weekend, where the occupants of an Antarctica research station discover an alien in a block of ice and then fight to stay alive as it consumes them one by one. Straight after that, it's the remake. Honestly, if it's not one Thing it's another.

I went to the casino and spent £2000 on chips. They were still frying at five in the morning.

I won a competition to meet my favourite 70s dare devil stunt man. Unfortunately I missed the train, and when I got there, he'd gone. I thought typical: speak, see and hear no Evel.

She said, the bed's not made yet, darling. I said, no but it will be one day. You should hear it play that guitar.

When the woman next door ran out of multi-surface cleaner, I said she could have mine. I gave her my Pledge.

I was going to have quick soak peas for tea. Then I remembered: I had a bath last night.

I called the taxi place. I said, do you have a screwdriver? He said, have you tried B&Q? I said, no, I didn't think they'd be interested in chauffeuring officers to and from the nick.

There was this jar of condiment in the cafe, singing Thin Lizzy songs. I thought, whey hey, rock salt.

I'm a bit wary of the new supervisor at the charcoal factory. If you ask me, he's a right shady character.

I said, doctor, every time I put a toe near water, I start to panic. He said, you've got dip-fearia.

My back door is notorious for sticking. I'm afraid it's not over adventurous when it comes to pontoon.

I bought my son a microscope and we spent endless hours scrutinising the marvels of the insect world. He said, this is brill, isn't it, Daddy? I said, not half, it's the bee's knees.

My car has a small stream running through it. It's a Ford.

This bloke told me he lived high in the sky, where the birds sing with a distinctive two-note call before laying their eggs in the nests of others. I thought, he's living in cloud cuckoo land.

I turned up at the pub in my swimming trunks. I said, alright, where's the pool table?

When I won Euro Millions, I treated myself to a new golf club. It's called St Andrews.

I once played cricket in the lingerie shop. I was caught in the slips.

The carpet's worn out. Lord knows what it gets up to when we're not in.

I know this kid whose parents are composed entirely of mud and water. He's a right son of a ditch.

My new girlfriend loves music but never sings. She's a humming bird.

I went in a charity shop. They said I could have it if I wanted.

I went in the pub next. They said I could have that as well. It was a free house.

Mrs Jones went to pay her council tax with a £10 note stuffed in each ear. The woman behind the counter said, here she comes, look, twenty pound in arrears again.

I keep driving my car into walls. I always make sure the cost of repairs outstrips my income, meaning I haven't any money left for food. You guessed it: I'm on a crash diet.

If you didn't see the match last night, it was about an inch and a half long, with a pink, phosphorus head.

I said, doctor, I keep spitting up small, grape-like objects. They always come in pairs and are filled with seeds. He said, you've got beriberi.

I wonder what the residents of Coronation Street watch on ITV Monday, Thursday and Friday at 7.30?

Is a choreographer an expert on Coronation Street?

I was walking past this research laboratory when a chair came crashing through the window. It must have been a mad scientist.

For anyone interested, there's a raunchy film on tonight, BBC1 at two o'clock: Closedown.

I was once married to two women at the same time. I don't know why. It just seemed really bigamy at the time.

It was a disappointing night at the constipation society AGM. Not a single motion was passed.

I went into this pizza shop. I ordered a box of stuffed-crust dominoes.

A goat has moved in two doors down. It's the new kid on the block.

I fell in love with a girl from Moscow. I was going to ask her to marry me, but didn't want to Russia.

First alien: I might build a secret base on Earth and another on Mars. Second alien: That's always been your trouble. You want the best of both worlds.

I saw a small horse, pulling a rabbit out of a hat. Next day, it did exactly the same, and the same again the day after that. It was a one trick pony.

I live in a spare tyre. Inner tube to be precise.

Next week, I'm moving into a flat.

My brother's Frank. He always speaks his mind.

When I was in Glasgow, I saw four blue bottles, playing drums and guitars. Someone said it was McFly.

I was working at the undertakers when they fetched this bloke in who had been chopped into a million pieces by a combine harvester. We did our best for him, naturally, and I'm proud to say I put the final toe nail in the coffin.

The short order cook at the hotel where I work is always mixing it up. He's a right stir fry.

I went in a pub and ordered a pint of PG Tips. He said, what, no beer? I said, no thanks, I'm tea total.

I used to be a mod. I must have been off my rocker.

My girlfriend has the same name as famous airline, Cathay Pacific. Well, nearly. Her first name is Kathy. It's her surname that's the problem. They call her Smith.

I was desperate for the toilet whilst visiting a famous west London football club. Queue. Pee. Aaah!

Two down with ten minutes to go, City sent the sub on. I thought, let's see how United cope with a nuclear powered hunter-killer.

I'm emigrating to Central Asia with my girlfriend. No one else. Just us. Becky. Stan.

I had a tooth crowned yesterday. It's the king of my mouth.

When I was in hospital, a surgeon removed my spine and replaced it with one half the size. He thinks that's the end of it but no chance. Mark my words: I'll get my own back one day.

I went to Ireland. I said, can I hire your country for a month, please?

The 11th Century ship discovered at the bottom of the North Sea is of Viking descent. According to Scandinavian wreck hordes, anyway...

As lightning illuminated the kitchen over and over, I discovered a bottle of ruby tucked away at the back of the cupboard. Not my usual tipple, but any port will do in a storm.

I really enjoy my job, mucking out, and my favourite film is Apocalypse Now. I love the smell of the pig farm in the morning.

Dancing the cha-cha slide is a nightmare. I kept falling in the teapot.

I phoned this sparky. I said, your advert boasts no job too small? Well, can you pop round and put me a new light bulb in?

Umpteen pieces of string and twine went on a night out. They all got a round in...except for the tight rope.

I followed signs for free parking. When I got there, it was this woman, giving away slices of spicy ginger cake.

People misunderstand me when I tell them I'm too tired. I was born with wheels instead of feet.

I saw a stone, dressed up as Roy Wood from Wizard. I thought, whey hey, glam rock.

I finally confronted the wife over her obsession with Alvin Stardust. She told me to wind my neck in: it was just my jealous mind.

There was this sign saying, cash paid for scrap. I said, I'll be back in five minutes with my boxing gloves.

We had a mouse at work, so the pest control man set traps all over the office. Next morning, we'd caught twenty-two of the infernal things, all on desks adjacent computers.

I went in the water and my cough and cold symptoms disappeared instantly. It was the vitamin sea.

Funny noises were coming from the hen house: boing-cluck-cluck, boing-cluck-cluck. The farmer said not to worry. It was just a spring chicken.

I roll my cigarettes. I take them to the top of this big hill and push them to the bottom.

I went to a hand car wash. I had my hands scrubbed by a Skoda Octavia.

My brother went missing and turned up on Jupiter. I always said he was on a different planet.

On the liqueur aisle in Tesco, I was shocked to see how many bottles were reserved for some bloke called Bailey.

My bride-to-be isn't half playing up because I arrived home late and missed the wedding rehearsal. She says she doesn't know where she stands with me.

White arrows in the road: anyone who thinks they are direction indicators is way off the mark. They're signs, fallen off the side of the Wrigley's Spearmint Gum lorry.

Double yellow lines: it's the trail left by giant slugs on a road race.

I went in this shop. I said, can I have a pet for my car? He said, I beg your pardon? I said, that's what you sell, isn't it? Carpets?

I left the cough mixture lid off and next morning it was filled with dead blue bottles. Talk about a Veno's fly trap.

I was driving off in my new car when I broke down. I thought, I'll never keep up the repayments.

I had a row with the wife, packed my case, then grabbed the dog, my Xbox, IPhone, iPad and iPod, and stormed out, not stopping until I reached John O'Groats. When I got back, a week later, she said, that's you all over, isn't it? You always have to take things too far.

When I divorced my wife, she took everything, house, car, money, even the dog. She was the one that got her way.

Every night's a night on the tiles for me. I'm a cat burglar.

I said, Jumbo sausage and chips, fifty-five times, please. The assistant said, are you sure you will eat all that? I said, it's not for me. It's for my elephant.

I saw a sign saying, hippodrome. Next thing, a flying hippo came in to land.

I went sledging in Scandinavia. I was in the Aussie cricket team that beat Norway by an innings and 879 runs.

That German barber near me is a real dab hand. If you need him, his name is Herr Cut.

I saw a pig, pruning a privet. I thought, ooh look, a hedge hog.

Just before the pub shut, I ordered Thai spring rolls, prosciutto melon and a cheese board. It was last hors d'oeuvres.

I've just been watching Steven Hawking's Universe. It was a really good programme, but I didn't know he owned it.

I was travelling at the speed of light when my car smashed through a computer screen and came to a screeching halt in a living room in Swansea. That's the last time you'll catch me on the information super highway.

That housewarming party I went to certainly lived up to its billing. The kitchen caught fire.

I was working in the store electrical department when a disgruntled customer came in, dripping water. He said, these floodlights you sold me...

I followed a sign saying, goods vehicle testing station. When I got there, it was this big lorry, giving a railway station a maths examination.

A bloke at the ornithology club asked me to name the most common bird in Iceland. I said, frozen chicken.

I said, doctor, my chest feels like it's on fire and I've got flames shooting up my throat. He said, you've got heartburn.

Egg in frying pan: Warm in here, isn't it? Sausage: I didn't know eggs could talk...

I bought a chocolate teapot. It was about as useful as a chocolate teapot.

What would you rather bee or a wasp?

I paid a visit to the Royal Philharmonic. I said to this trumpet, do you get much female attention? It said, nothing like as much as my mate in percussion. Honestly, he's a right sex cymbal.

I hear the Royal Philharmonic slipped out of their hotel at midnight to avoid paying the bill. Orchestral manoeuvres in the dark.

I saw a medium sized, burrowing mammal, wearing bovver boots and knuckle dusters. It was a haard-vark.

There was this woman in the park with a set of goalposts on her head. Someone said her name was Annette.

I bought a head and shoulders picture of the glamour model formerly known as Jordan. It was half price.

William Wallace and his compatriots must have had terrible skin in the film Braveheart. Who can forget the bit where Wallace raised his sword and said, they make take our lives...but they'll never take our Free Derm.

I said, doctor, I can't stop watching Beau Geste. I've seen it 318 times this month alone. He said, hmmm, it sounds like Legionnaire's disease.

I was filling in an application form and had to provide the names of two referees. I eventually plumped for Howard Webb and Pierre Luigi Collina.

Howard Webb gave me a lift in his new car. I said, what's that fancy button on the dash, Howard? He said, that's my trip recorder.

Spiderman is really a premiership referee. The clue's in the name: it's Howard Webb.

I saw two DAB radios, playing tennis. I thought, ooh look, radioactivity.

Norman hates William. He's Billy Norm hates.

Every time there's an argument in our house, my mother sides with my brother, Gabriel. Honestly, she thinks he's a right little angel.

My driving instructor told me off for being in the wrong gear. I said, what did you expect? Helmet and gloves, and fire-resistant overalls?

He told me to ease off the accelerator and depress the clutch. I said, OK, accelerator, you're not a bad old stick. Clutch, you make for lousy gear changes. Oh, and in case you're wondering, that gooey, smelly stuff on my shoe, it's dog pooh.

I passed a car with the Complete Works of Keats on the parcel shelf. It was poetry in motion.

My friend has a six-pack. He's also terribly boring. His name is Abdul.

His brother also has a six-pack. He's also terribly boring but worse. His name is Abdullah.

Thieves broke into a pet shop in Doncaster last night. Police found a metal chain, tied round a lamppost. They think it might be a lead.

I started watching This is Your Life but turned it off after ten minutes. I didn't get mentioned once.

That Phil O'Delphia must be some guy. He's got a whole city named after him.

I wouldn't say I'm weedy. But my nickname is Mr Puniverse.

When my uncle won the lottery, he gave everyone in the family a million pounds each. I was the only one who missed out. Not that I'm surprised. I've always been the poor relation.

I can't believe it: a kid I was at school with has just been on tele to announce he's discovered a planet only two miles in circumference. Talk about a small world.

There was this crow with red, yellow and blue feathers. It was sporting the latest parrot fashions.

My brother-in-law's turned into a right snob since he grew a fringe down to his chin. I'm sick of him walking about with his nose in the hair.

I was in a yellow cab, heading vertically up the side of the Empire State Building, with an Irish cabbie that wouldn't stop talking. I thought, blimey O'Reilly, this guy is driving me up the wall.

As we headed down the other side, I thought I'd ask if he'd spent his entire life in New York, or had he been abroad? He said, no, mister, I've never been a woman.

I set this tuft of grass to work, doing odd jobs round the house, but nothing got finished. It was a right lazy sod.

I got my first big break while I was in the navy. I ran an aircraft carrier aground, putting it out of service for two years.

I had this awful cough so the wife rubbed my chest with Vic. It cured my cough, but I came out in an awful rash from his stubbly chin.

What's yellow and wears plimsolls? A banana, I was making the plimsolls bit up.

I work part-time at Aintree, looking after nags on Grand National day. It's not the best job I've ever had, but, hey ho, horses for courses.

I popped in car supermarket the other day. It was full of cars, pushing trolleys, doing their weekly shop.

I won't be revisiting the air museum in a hurry. It was full of old wigs.

I said, doctor, I'm convinced I was a Spitfire during the war. He said, ex-plane yourself...

I rang this free phone number. I said, can you send me an iPhone's 4 in white, please?

The sign outside the restaurant said: kids eat free. When we got inside, it was full of juvenile goats.

I used to go out with a female chiropodist. She was a real fun gal.

I need someone to fix my boiler, but everyone I've called is Corgi registered. That's no good to me: I own a Dalmatian.

What's the Bee Gees favourite television mini-series? Band of Brothers.

There was this overweight bloke, punching himself in the stomach. I asked what he was doing. He said, fighting the flab.

I can see for miles out of my bedroom window. Which is really odd, because Miles is the chap next door.

It's going to be really windy on Tuesday. It's national mushy peas day.

I watched a couple of legal documents having a fight. Talk about a battle of wills.

My wife is an axe murderer. An axe upset her one day, so she grabbed it by the handle and threw it off the edge of a cliff.

I hear the incredible hulk has opened a shop in West Bromwich. Word is it's a green grocer's.

A bar of Aero has launched a pop career. Its stage name is Michael Bubble.

Madonna. I'm mad on her.

I was doing brilliant in the pub quiz until question 15: who had a hit with the very best of Rod Stewart? How was I supposed to know? I wasn't born until 1989.

When I was in prison, I reported a fault with my cell door. There was no handle on the inside.

I received a letter through the post yesterday, offering me a free trial. I turned it down. Knowing my luck, they'd only find me guilty.

I went to buy some new tyres. The bloke said, Goodyear? I said, not bad. Now, how about the tyres?

My optician lives on Shredded Wheat. He's fibre optic.

I got a call from the wife to tell me the computer had crashed. I said, you what? I didn't even know it had sent for its licence.

I opened my laptop and found it covered in gelatinous pork shoulder. Something needs doing about all this spam.

I went to the pub yesterday and got drunk. What I need to work out now is whose belly I'm in.

Cobras and Pythons. They lead a charmed life.

I said, you're holding your biro upside down. He said, what's it got to do with you? I said, look, you're missing the point...

I visited Edinburgh Castle and found it filled with soldiers in short skirts. It was the military tutu.

A bloke offered me £200 for my pet alligator. It snapped his hand off.

I filled up at a shell garage. The cashier was a snail.

Last Christmas, I bought BMX's for the kids and I'm still paying them off twelve months later. Honestly, I'm caught up in a right cycle of debt.

I said, doctor, I've come out in an itchy rash which has started laying eggs. He said, you've got chicken pox.

I hated my job at the call centre so much that I chopped up all the communication equipment with a machete. I was arrested for phone hacking.

A friend of mine was trampled underfoot at the races. He's currently in hospital and his condition is described as stable.

Hot tip for the 2.35 at Kempton Park: Dusty Carpet, never been beaten.

I've just seen a stringed, musical instrument, floating past my bedroom window. It must have been one of those air guitars.

I applied for a job as an illustrator but didn't even get an interview. Oh well, back to the drawing board...

My wife says all I do is lounge around, watching football, and if our marriage is to survive the weekend, we need to make time to talk. I thought, yeah, right: like that's going to happen when I've just settled down to enjoy extended highlights of Rotherham United versus Bury in the second round of the Johnstone's Paint Trophy.

I saw this car, covered in pasta strings and tomato sauce. It was coming from the direction of spaghetti junction.

News at Ten came on. Trevor McDonald said: these are tonight's headlines. And the camera zoomed in on his forehead.

I went to a jar of Kenco's funeral. Talk about coffee mourning.

A bank robber was speeding towards me and my mate with a car full of stolen cash. I said, I think he's trying to drive a wedge between us.

Have you seen all the Yorkshire puddings in Tesco? That Aunt Bessie must be a real workaholic.

Ben and Jerry are just as bad.

I managed to get my self assessment form in on time: short, stocky build, going thin on top and getting on a bit.

I couldn't believe it when my bedtime drink began blowing up balloons and performing party tricks. It was Cocoa the clown.

I put Zulu on, but instead of all action, all I got was a fly on the wall documentary about a toilet attendant at Chester Zoo.

Bet you didn't know there's a city in France which only has a couple of public toilets? It's Toulouse.

A delivery driver turned up with my wife's birthday present gripped between his thighs. That's the last time I order anything on loin.

I'm giving up my flat near the university after discovering my car bashed in and covered with corned beef hash. It's the second time in a week I've had trouble with stew dents.

I stopped for petrol and found staff and customers hitting tennis balls over a net. It was a service station.

I'd tell you a joke about butter. But you might spread it.

I was driving down the motorway when a hearse whizzed by on the inside. Flipping undertakers.

I've just seen a car driven by a pig. It was hogging the middle lane.

This sign said, queuing traffic. When I got there, it was loads of cars, playing snooker.

I keep thinking I'm an ostrich. I know it's not normal and I'm going to have to face up to my problem sooner or later. I can't keep burying my head in the sand.

I was only a week old when a kid in the next cot tried to sell me a dodgy rattle. I said, do you think I was born yesterday?

I ordered a Suzuki online. When it was delivered, I said, that's not a motorbike, it's a flipping key to the zoo. This bloke covered in elephant pooh stuttered, yeah, it's a z-zoo key.

Is a space bar where astronauts go for a drink?

I heard this quack-quack noise coming from the bathroom. It was the toilet duck.

Robotics. It's R2D2 with hiccups.

I started work in a cotton factory and was mesmerised by this woman who did nothing but turn round in circles all day. It was spinning Jenny.

I knew my job at the fishmongers wouldn't last long. My sole wasn't in it.

The wife said I was crazy buying a pneumatic drill. She didn't think there was anything wrong with the old one.

It was freezing cold in NatWest today. It must have been a banker's draft.

I found a toilet in a field. It was pot luck.

My sister's marriage to the subsidence engineer is in trouble. I can't say I'm surprised. I could see the cracks appearing months ago.

My sister isn't the only one. That nice couple who operate the lighthouse: their marriage is on the rocks as well.

I spent June, July and August in prison with Bananarama. We wrote a song about our experiences. It's called gruel summer.

Cannibals. They'll make your blood boil.

I've been asked to submit an article for an online discussion. Unfortunately I've nothing forum.

There's a big meeting next week for those Corby trouser wrinkle remover contraptions kept in hotel rooms. It's a press conference.

I went to the doctors. I said, every time I buy a book, I'm only interested in the last few pages. He said, it sounds like appendixitis.

I went on holiday with my uncles and their wives. When the ladies luggage went missing, I lent them both a pair of my trousers. Talk about aunts in my pants.

The dangerous dogs act clearly isn't working. I've just seen a bull terrier, plate spinning, and it broke the lot.

I went on The Apprentice, and Lord Sugar sent me to the stores for a left-handed screwdriver and a long stand. I came back three hours later with a tin of Tartan paint.

I went on the German Apprentice next. I got feuered.

I auditioned for the X-Factor and they packed me straight off to boot camp. I thought, oh my God, I've just joined the marines.

My Glaswegian boss has put a cap on my earnings. When I get my wage packet, it comes complete with Tam O'Shanter.

I was on the dairy aisle when a lump of cheddar poked its tongue out at me. I thought, that's not very mature.

Automatic gearboxes: not on my shift.

I wish my wife wouldn't take things so literally. I asked her to turn the television on, and she began dancing seductively on the hearth rug.

City's new centre forward is extremely comfortable on the ball. He's currently fast asleep in the penalty area, using it as a pillow.

I was admiring boats in Malaga harbour when they all started laughing at me. I thought, whey hey, it's the Spanish ha-ha-mada.

I went to Lord's cricket ground and found it filled with rats and cockroaches. It was the first day of the pest match.

The new park bowling green is an absolute disgrace...according to a mole.

I've got a hole in my sock. Darn it.

I saw a swordfight on the way into work. It was on a duel carriageway.

When I left prison, I was shocked to see that former cellmate, infamous criminal Carlos the Jackal, had mentioned me in his autobiography. I thought, crikey, I'm in the bad books now.

I tried my hand at landscape gardening. But I can't say I pulled any trees up.

I broke into Sea World and nicked the star attraction. If anyone's thinking of asking what I did with it, don't bother: my lips are sealed.

When I met my wife, she was on the tele. She worked in Comet and had just seen a mouse.

I'm reading a book on oil exploration. What a bore...

I always listen to Radio 4 down the cellar: underneath the Archers.

I arrived home egged and gored after being attacked whilst short-cutting through the farm. Not that the wife seemed concerned. She thought it was a right cock and bull story.

Five o'clock shadow: I've beard it all before

I was on holiday, sunbathing next to my friend the plastic surgeon. But not for long: half an hour later, he'd melted.

I love gardening, but can't say I thought much of Channel 4 programme, Cutting Edge.

Every year on VE night, a ghostly world war two canine appears at the foot of my bed. It's the bulldog spirit.

I work as a private tutor. It's not the best job I've ever had but, hey ho, another day, another scholar.

It was mad busy at the petrol station. It was all hands to the pump.

I've got a frog in my throat. I've just swallowed a Frenchman.

A friend of mine tried eating himself to death on Chinese takeaways. It was attempted chop-suey-cide.

I went to see four lumps of iron in concert. It was a heavy metal band.

My posh wife said she needed a new hobby. I said, find one, then. She said, I'm glad you said that. I'm divorcing you.

I've finally landed a job with no pressure. I mend broken water mains.

I used to be a door to door salesman. I sold doors to doors.

When the doctor wasn't looking, I poured cough mixture into his coffee. I thought it was about time he had a taste of his own medicine.

I work in a cholesterol tablet factory in New York. It's on Statin Island.

I did my GCSE's on a ski slope. Talk about a steep learning curve.

When I was a literary agent, I received a submission from some bloke called Charles Dickens. I thought, no way. Then I realised: he was a ghost writer.

I was a bit peeved with the Money Supermarket website. There wasn't so much as a penny on BOGOF.

Dorothy Gale and Almira Gulch in The Wizard of Oz? Which is witch?

I engaged in a spot of impromptu DIY when my television went on the blink, but finished up with a massive electric shock for my endeavours. Ooh, megahertz!

Woolly Mammoths. They're a bit long in the tooth.

I went for an interview for a street cleaner's job. I said, will I need to go on any training courses? He said, no, you just pick it up as you go along.

I was back-heeled at the races by a horse that finished twenty third in a field of twenty three. Honestly, it felt like I'd been kicked by a donkey.

Breaking news: a presenter from I'm a Celebrity Get Me out of Here has been mobbed by ecstatic girl fans, whilst relaxing on a Mediterranean cruise. Apparently it was all hands on Dec.

When I was in the army, I was in B Company. We all wore yellow and black hooped sweaters.

I was at the funfair with my mates when this eight foot bloke appeared, gathered everyone together, and started reciting, one potato, two potato, three potato, four, five potato, six potato, seven potato, more. It was the big dipper.

Blooming speed cameras are everywhere nowadays. I only had 3 points on my licence. Then I bought a Scalextric.

I was born on the moors. My friends call me Peat.

If you see me out and about with a bloke with ladder rungs instead of legs, don't worry. It's only my step father.

I went on holiday to Spain, while my brother chose Portugal. We always were on a different plane.

I saw a snake, chalking sums on a blackboard. I thought it was an adder at first. But it couldn't have been, because it got them all wrong.

My Grandmother plays for Manchester United. She's Nanny.

I saw a writing pad, working out at the gym. I thought, ooh look, an exercise book.

I said, doctor, I can't stop sighing with relief. He said, you're obviously a man of phew words.

The local plumbers' merchant has fallen upon hard times...according to a leaked memo.

I've got a drink problem. I can't hit my mouth with the glass.

A girl just caught my eye. I have a glass one and it came out on the number 22 bus.

I was at a dwarves' birthday party when it all kicked off outside in the street. Police have the entire incident captured on CCTV. Fortunately for me, I'm above suspicion.

My friend Harvey makes his living hanging pictures. His surname is Wallbanger.

I made a plaster-cast model of Chewbacca from Star Wars, but must have got the mix wrong, because within a couple of days it began to disintegrate. Never mind: I suppose it's just the way the Wookie crumbles.

I'm taking a diploma in aeronautical engineering. Why not? I mean, it's not exactly rocket science, is it?

A sign in HMV said: door alarmed. I thought, no wonder with Exorcist the Director's Cut playing in loop on the adjacent aisle.

I went to the video store. I said, do you have Men in Black? He said, surely you must have noticed security by the door?

My friend has a flock of seagulls nesting on his head. He has another load in his ears, and some more up his nostrils. Ah, poor old Cliff...

I went to the post office and mailed myself home in a padded envelope. I was bouncing around in the back of a van when my mobile rang. It was the wife, all in a tiz, wanting to know where I'd got to. I said, calm down, darling. I'll be back in a jiffy.

There was this bird in my garden. It had movie star good looks and was making a noise like a paper bag. I thought, whey hey, it's Rustle crow.

I said, please, please, *please*, don't let me turn out like you. I was begging to differ.

I've just been awarded exclusive rights to distribute property board games in Outer Mongolia. I've got the Monopoly.

My maths teacher said, if you had $32,000 in one hand and $32,000 in the other, how much would you have? I thought, that's the $64,000 question.

I've never been lucky. Then I was captured by cannibals, who immediately put me between two pieces of bread. Now, for the first time in my life, I'm on a roll.

I saw this great white, counting out fivers on a doorstep. I thought, ooh look, a loan shark.

I saw an Alsatian with horns yesterday. Or was it a bull dog?

Walking past the farm, I heard singing coming from the chicken coop. I thought, they'll never make it on the eggs factor.

I answered a bedsitter advert then spent the next two years changing nappies for a bunk-bed.

I've just seen a fruit stall, crying its eyes out. I thought, dear oh dear, someone's upset the apple cart.

I've just resigned from my gritter driver's job. Humberside county council have asked me to reconsider, but I've told them no chance. Hull can freeze over first.

I've been on a city break with my pals. For your information, London is now in eighteen pieces and spread across fourteen counties.

Judging by the size of the garden wall, I wouldn't have fancied paying the council tax on Hadrian's house!

I caught my nephew, swinging from a chandelier while eating a banana. I thought, well I'll be a monkey's uncle.

That cub with the bow tie, the one who hangs around with Yogi Bear, did you know he's taken up football? Unfortunately he's not very good. Last time I watched him play, he got Boo-Booed off the pitch.

I went outside and found my car on bricks. Someone said this 70s pop group were to blame. Apparently it was Stealers Wheel.

People can say or do what they want to me nowadays. All I do is grin stupidly in return: I've lost my temper.

I ran someone over with my combine harvester but he got the blame. He's currently out on bale.

I've changed my name by deed poll. Officially, I'm now known as P136CTH. But my friends just call me Reg.

A friend of mine strangled a Smurf then fled the scene before the police arrived. Talk about getting away with blue murder.

I ate myself for dinner yesterday. But I'm still here, look. Still, they say you are what you eat, don't they?

The captain shouted, abandon ship. I felt really stupid when I ran on deck in my lifebelt and flippers, and everyone else was dancing away to Cliff Richard and The Shadows.

I went on a caveman's stag do. We went clubbing.

Wayne Rooney missed a penalty, so I ran on the pitch, broke his legs then pushed the goalposts over. Mum sent me straight to bed and put my Subbuteo back in the cupboard.

I went to the bottle bank. The cashier's name was Stella.

I've just bought shares in an underwear company. I've got a vested interest.

This OAP gave me his takeaway leftovers. My mate said, what's that you're eating? I said, just a chip off the old bloke.

I went on Jeremy Kyle when I found out my girlfriend had been cheating. I don't think he was too impressed when I explained it was during a game of Monopoly.

I hate work. I might eat the tax office next.

All I eat is Arrow T-50s, 5/16, 8mm: they're my staple diet.

I was on the toiletry aisle when tablets of Lifebuoy, Imperial Leather and Cussons Mild Cream simultaneously began singing songs from HMS Pinafore. I thought, whey hey, a soap opera.

My Aunty Fiona once stole this big, American state. I can recall the newspaper headline like it was yesterday: Fi Nicks Arizona.

She got off in the end, but was back in court soon after, accused of trying to sell a space telescope to an unsuspecting Japanese tourist. I remember thinking, no way. It's not Fi's Hubble.

There was a huge tailback on the motorway. I think it was Godzilla's.

I gave up my job as a dog sleigh handler. It was getting too mush-mush for me.

I was driving down the road and came across this sign saying, blind summit. When I got there, it was twenty delegates, sitting round a table, all reading Braille.

I've resigned from my zoo-keeper's job because the new star attraction is getting on my nerves. I refuse to panda to that obnoxious black and white bear one second longer.

Just my luck. I put the tele on and it didn't fit.

I arrived at the hunting shop, pressed on the handle and found myself hanging upside down in a net. It was a trap door.

I saw a party of poodles on their way into a Chinese restaurant. Talk about dog eat dog.

The label on the trousers said, 32 leg. I thought, crikey, that would fit four octopuses.

I bought a houseplant. Two years later, it had blossomed into a beautiful, three-bedroomed semi-detached.

That new skyscraper near me: too many flaws.

I phoned this helpline. A bloke said, seven sevens are forty-nine. Add twelve, takeaway six, equals fifty-five. It was the Sumaritans.

Sumo wrestlers. They're big in Japan.

I used to think I worked in a sandpaper factory. Then someone explained we were making maps of the desert.

The former NASA scientist who claimed we're on a collision course with the sun has hardly set the world on fire with his theory.

I've just been watching the 2012 Cumbrian sheep dog trials. All in all, 177 dogs were found guilty.

There's this city in Mali named after a referee called Timothy with a preference for handing out yellow cards in pairs. It's Timbuktu.

I'm going undercover to expose corrupt referees. You guessed it: I'm a whistle blower.

This sign said, please take your litter home. I thought, how silly is that? As if cats can read.

I rang BT Vision. They said to try Specsavers.

TV guides: I'm sick of them leading expeditions round the back of the tele.

I used to be an owl. Do I care? Not really. In actual fact, I don't give a hoot.

The psychics round me are such a miserable bunch, I always end up walking out before the end of the session. But never mind, eh? I suppose I'll find a happy medium one day.

I was in borstal, sharing a dormitory with twenty chavs. Talk about all the mod cons.

I got into an argument with a streaker. He was all mouth and no trousers.

Candles. They get on my wick.

I've joined this organisation where no one knows anyone's name, and all we do all day is go out and get drunk. It's called alcoholics anonymous.

My name is Jerzy. I come from Warsaw. I enrolled at the Polish club in Barnsley. But my first visit was definitely my last. It was filled with English people, drooling over tins of Kiwi cherry blossom and bottles of Car Plan T-cut.

I asked my boss at the coffee shop for a bonus. He said, perk you later.

My wife and I went to the doctors when we woke one morning to find ourselves covered in Velcro. He said not to worry. It was a very rare condition, but everything would be alright. All we needed to do was stick together.

I was really looking forward to my holiday to the Middle East. Unfortunately it was no great sheikh.

I went to a party dressed as Sir Lancelot and didn't get in till dawn. Talk about night in shining armour.

Did you hear about the chocolate brownie? She went to summer camp and melted.

I said to the River Ouse, what's the capital of Finland? I was testing the water...

This bloke tried to sell me a mountain. I told him it was a bit steep.

I celebrated becoming a lottery millionaire by having the winning numbers tattooed across my forehead: big mistake. Everywhere I went, people were saying, take that luck off your face.

I'm on the plane tomorrow. I'm taking two inches off the bottom of the door.

Did you hear about the fight between the rugby field and the football field? It was a right pitched battle.

I got a call from this head hunter, saying he wanted to meet me to discuss a job opportunity. When I got there, it was a trick. He tried to cut my head off and chased me down the street with a spear.

I caught my lower forearm, collating information on bomb making equipment. I didn't mess around. I got straight on the phone to the terror wrist hotline.

We're having a cricket match on Shrove Tuesday. The toss is at one o'clock.

I spat my dummy out yesterday. I almost swallowed a mannequin.

My brother is addicted to online gambling. He's currently hanging upside down on the washing line, talking to the bookies.

I was born without a body. No chest. No arms. No legs. Nothing. But it wasn't all bad news. When I started school, I was immediately installed as head boy.

I dreaded Christmas and birthdays, mind. All I got was blooming caps.

Sometimes people would buy me a toothbrush. But all that stopped the day I had my teeth out.

My kid brother fared even worse. When he was born, he only had an ear. I remember asking Mum if he would lead a normal life. She said, I'm afraid not: he's deaf.

I was in a competition to see who could last longest in the desert without a drink. I won thirst prize.

OK, so I went to Spain and forgot my sun tan oil. No need to rub it in.

I was starving when I arrived at the concert. So I ate the act. It was Meatloaf.

I was at a friend's house when a procession of men in uniforms galloped up the staircase on ceremonial horses. Apparently it was the household cavalry.

Did you hear about the man who slept continuously for seventy-seven years? It was the rest of his life.

I went for a job as a trainee cobbler. He said, have you ever soled shoes? I said, yeah, I used to work in the footwear department of House of Fraser.

I mixed butter with sugar, 4 eggs, vanilla extract, milk and self raising flour. Then I baked the lot in the oven for half an hour at gas mark 4. Piece of cake.

My wife insisted upon calling our new puppy Riverfern Tequila Sunset. I thought, talk about giving a dog a bad name.

I made a push-bike out of old medicines. I got arrested for drug pedalling.

Jonathon Ross is being blackmailed by a sea bird, purporting to be his long-lost brother, Albert Ross.

I'm taking a degree in criminology. Part one is the study of serial killers. I can't wait for my first Hannibal lecture.

I saw this bloke, running down the road with a door strapped to his back. I thought, he's unhinged.

Dog fouling round our way is really getting out of hand. I was clean through on goal yesterday when I was tripped from behind by a rampaging Rottweiler.

I saw a novel, sending messages on a mobile phone. Or at least I thought it was a novel. Then I realised: it was a text book.

I've just seen a bull with a runny nose. It was a right snotty cow.

I asked the wife what her favourite album was. She said, I quite like his, that Shearer bloke on Match of the Day.

I saw this sign saying, local shops. What a swizz. When I got there, they were absolutely crammed with full fat foods.

Two blue-bottles went fly fishing...

I went to buy a new car with the wife. I said to the salesman, gobble-gobble, gobble-gobble, to which he replied, gobble-gobble, gobble-gobble. The wife said, what was all that about? I said, we were just talking turkey.

NatWest, Barclays and Lloyds were all checking in for the 1.30 to Palma. I thought, ooh look, bank holidays.

I went to the travel agents. I said, I want to go all exclusive. She said, don't you mean all inclusive? I said, no, exclusive. I want to become famous then sell my story for a mint.

My wife's been on page 3 for years now. She says it's the worst book she's ever read.

I was leafing through my old school photos when a ball of phlegm clobbered me in the face. It was a spitting image.

I used to be a lieutenant. I lived in a toilet.

Negotiations for the new market place have now stalled.

I rang this plumber. I said, it says fully vetted in your advert. I don't doubt you've had your annual injections, but have you been wormed as well?

I rang a personal injury specialist. I said, how much to break someone's legs, mate?

1960's East End mob rule. It was all the Krays.

I went Christmas shopping in Toy Town. I broke the bank.

I tried a night out in Bakewell. Never again. It was full of tarts.

Did you hear about the short-tongued lorry driver, who spilled his load of shirts and trousers across the motorway? He clothed the road.

I was installing new computers in the stock exchange. I said to this chap, spec' you later? He said, not me, mate. I'm just the cleaner.

There was this bloke, holed up in a house and threatening to shoot anyone who came near. Next thing, a policeman turned up with his sleeves ablaze. He said, alright, who called fire arms?

I phoned the National Trust. I said, I understand you can keep a secret...?

I saw a group of King Edwards in police uniform. I thought, whey hey, potato peelers.

There was this bloke in Red Indian headdress, driving a big, red engine, with flashing blue lights on top. Apparently it was the chief fire officer.

I said, doctor, I've a little red lump on my eye that keeps going oink-oink. He said, it's a pig stye.

If anyone fancies a free iPad, I've heard they're giving them away at A&E.

I was walking through the woods when I spotted mum, dad and 2.4 children, perched on the uppermost branches of a silver birch. I thought, aww look, a family tree...

For my girlfriend's birthday, I bought her this huge reservoir, filled with water, and supported by a reinforced concrete wall. She said, darling, that's beautiful. I didn't think you gave a dam.

I shared my ideas with a bloke at the pub, who showed his appreciation by treating me to a slap up meal. Talk about food for thought.

Walking through the Scottish highlands at midnight, I spotted a large group of men in tartan, skulking around in the dark. It was clan destine.

I live in an Almshouse. If you ever pay me a visit, the back door's just above the elbow.

That thingamajig round your wrist that tells the time. Watchamacallit?

I went to B&Q for a couple of sheets of fine sandpaper but all they had was multi-packs. I thought, oh well, sometimes you have to take the rough with the smooth.

I saw sign saying, wet floor. So I emptied a bottle of water on it.

Did you hear about the blind cannibal with a foot fetish? He tried eating a tow truck.

I took to my heels yesterday. Who would have thought it? Little old me, falling in love with my shoes?

I hear street artist Banksy celebrated the birth of his new child in typical fashion. Apparently he painted the town red.

Everyone was in a foul mood at the market today: there was a grumble sale on.

I saw a blue bottle land in a tub of Lurpak. I thought, ooh look, a butterfly.

I went into a pound shop and put 17 items on the counter. I said, how much for this lot?

The British team were leading in the 4 x 400 metre international cake-makers challenge. Then they dropped the battenburg.

I went in the travel agents. I said, do you have any cheap flights? She sold me a set of darts.

I discovered three holes in the ground, each with buckets and a rope for drawing water. I thought, well, well, well...

Hurdles. Just take them in your stride.

I thought I was imagining things when I spotted a Red Admiral. What the Russian navy were doing in Marks and Spencer in Gateshead is beyond me.

I went to the Edinburgh Military Tattoo. I came home with 2 Para inked across my chest.

The M1 has been resurfaced with silk. Word is that traffic is flowing smoothly.

I'm very well-groomed. I've been married 86 times.

Algebra. I take a dim view of it.

I went to the fair and came away with the Earl of Cumberland. I won him on hook a Duke.

I had a go on the bumping cars next. It could only happen to me: I lost my no claims bonus.

There was this bloke, walking down the street, shaking his arms and littering the pavement with chocolate covered, caramel biscuit bars. He certainly had a few Twix up his sleeves.

I resigned from my job in the perfume shop. I was sick of people odouring me around.

My wife lost the diamond out of her ring during Sunday dinner. Now she sticks her head down the pot every time she goes to the toilet, convinced it will turn up eventually. I'm not so sure. Personally, I reckon she's just going through the motions.

I called a mobile hairdresser yesterday, and a Nokia E-series turned up with a pair of scissors.

The new couple next door both have devil-like horns. I've also seen them wearing red capes and carrying tridents. I thought, just my luck. Neighbours from hell.

I'm Liverpool's new first team coach. I'm racked out with seats and ferry the team to all its away matches.

I said, what's a matador? And this door said, my hinges need oiling.

Pennsylvania. It's the HB capital of the world.

The wife has fed me meat and vegetable casserole every night for a month now. Honestly, it's making me stewicidal.

I witnessed rival takeaway owners, Mr Lee and Mr Burgin, meet face to face during a midnight stroll. Neither said a word. They passed like chips in the night.

I went into this pie shop. I said, the square on the hypotenuse is equal to the squares on the other two sides added together.

My girlfriend put on quite a bit of weight prior to entering the beauty contest. During the interview round, she was asked which person in the world she most admired. She said, Mr Kipling.

I'd resign from my job at the action man factory tomorrow if didn't need the money. Unfortunately it looks like I'll just have to soldier on.

I went to Pizza Hut and ordered a stuffed crust Hawaiian with free refills. When I'd finished, I said, right, now where's the diesel pump?

Never look a gift horse in the mouth. I did and it bit my nose off.

I stopped at a greasy spoon cafe and ordered an all day breakfast. I started eating at 9 and didn't finish while 5.

Due to the state of the economy, Bob the Builder has unfortunately been made redundant. From now on, can everyone please refer to him as Robert, as he feels this would improve his future job prospects?

I saw a Nikon Coolpix S2550 doing 120mph in a Ferrari. I thought, ooh look, a speed camera.

I've just seen an eagle, reading a bible. It was a bird of pray.

This celebrity singer gave me a piggy back ride across the river. It was Bryan Ferry.

I was strolling through this Chinese restaurant with Fido, when a waiter came running up to me. He said, what you doing, mister? I said, calm down. I'm just taking the dog for a wok.

Customs officers. They're on your case.

I see they've been experimenting mixing haemoglobin with milk to make a new form of red cheese. I was privileged enough to visit the factory last week. It was blood curdling.

This bloke asked me if I knew where he could get a new wig from. I said, not off the top of my head.

I said to St George, you've never even seen a dragon. He said, don't patronise me.

St George's favourite pop group is Slade. The dragon hates them.

I won the world soapy bubble-making championships yesterday. See my latest blog for a blow by blow account.

I was on a road trip across the USA and gave a lift to this bloke, who couldn't stop scratching, and also claimed to be a mass murderer. He said, you've probably heard of me. They call me the Itcher...

A major leak has occurred at the ink factory. Locals are furious. They say it's a right blot on the landscape.

I went in this fishing tackle shop, and Pole called Rod sold me a reel.

I saw the Hunchback of Notre Dame on his way into the house of mirrors. I thought, things could get ugly here.

This cannibal wanted to know why footballers spit so much. I said, perhaps you leave them on the barbecue too long.

I lost my needle in a haystack. Trying to find it again was like trying to find a needle in a haystack.

The world plate spinning record, I've just smashed it.

I arrived at the pearly gates. I thought, heavens above.

I've lived and died six times now. Next time I'll be in seventh heaven.

I said, a packet of helicopter crisps, please. He said, I'm afraid I've just sold the last bag, sir. I said, OK, I'll have plane.

Did you hear about the football match in the Himalayas, refereed by Joe Pesquali? Talk about high pitched.

I've just seen a chocolate bar dressed in khaki and covered in medals. I think it was a war Aero.

I bought a hand grenade online. It cost me a bomb.

Decorating? I'd rather watch paint dry.

I'm a very small man who keeps going oink-oink. I'm a pig, me.

I went to the pub on Christmas day but all they were serving was boiled sweets. Bar, humbug.

I went on holiday to the Middle East and it absolutely poured it down. Bah, rain.

My hobby is visiting breakers-yards and taking pictures of old cars. I keep them in my scrap book.

I received two job offers on the same day, one on a production line and the other in a dismantling yard. It was make or break time.

I went to a bonfire and my mate's head exploded. Not that I was surprised. I always said he was a head banger.

The best bonfire competition was declared a draw. All entries were extremely well-matched.

Two boys were tugging at a car, one at the front and one at the back. It went from twenty foot to thirty foot, and then forty. Then I realised: it was a stretch limo'.

I made a citizen's arrest when I saw this bloke, walking down the road with WH Smith under his arm. The police charged him with shoplifting.

I've just seen two dictionary armies, preparing for battle. It was clearly a war of words.

My son was being really naughty on a visit to the apiary. I said, beehive.

I said, doctor, I've developed a peculiar talent. I can cut through wood using my neck. He said, you've got a saw throat.

It was the morning of my new job in the railway line factory. I was enjoying a hearty breakfast, when the wife said, hadn't you better be making tracks?

I was relaxing in the bath when an aircraft carrier and two frigates suddenly appeared in my naval...

Someone kept breaking wind at the New Year's Eve get together. It was obviously a party pooper.

I was woken last night by the sound of someone stealing my gates. Not that I said anything. They may have taken a fence.

My best friend is an odd job man. He specialises in floor-coverings and emulsioning ceilings. If you ever need him, just ask for Matt.

I opened a shop selling exercise books but closed it down after the first week. There was no margin in it.

My girlfriend and I had a fall out on the big wheel. After a while, I said, look, this is going nowhere. All we're doing is going round in circles.

I'm sick of next door's alarm going off. How it affords all these foreign holidays is beyond me.

It's just been announced that staff at the tape measure factory are working to rule.

Wyatt Earp, Pat Garrett and Wild Bill Hickok once put on an exhibition of original oil paintings. It was the world's first example of mixed marshal arts.

I had Thai sweet chilli last night. It was a tie, cut up into pieces, and covered in sweet chilli.

I used to be a PT instructor at the police training college. I'd say, give me twenty-five, and all the candidates would immediately collapse to the floor. Talk about laying the law down.

There's a man-eating chicken on the loose. Stay indoors. Don't hen danger yourself.

What's the coldest place in Britain? It's Brrrmingham.

I heard this noise coming towards me. It was going, brr, trickle, left-right, brr, trickle, left-right. It was the cold stream guards.

I said, doctor, every time that extreme magician bloke comes on the tele, I get shivers down my spine. He said, you've got chill Blaines.

I tried fobbing my careers advisor off by pretending I wanted to work in X-ray. No such luck. He saw straight through me.

My first cage fight ended in disaster. A hamster knocked me out in three seconds.

I bumped into this bloke yesterday with the Royal Oak, Alma, Horseshoe and Prince of Wales strung round his neck. It was a pub chain.

The irate judge hung a head out of the broken window. He said, I suppose you want this back, don't you? I said, it's up to you, mate. The ball's in your court.

I was walking along, minding my own business, when a Persian cat hit me on the back of the head. A Border Collie clobbered me next, then a Siamese and a Chihuahua. I thought, blimey, it's raining cats and dogs.

Perpetuate. It's a club for people who hate pet cats.

I was working on the fish counter when this bloke walked in and machine-gunned the display. I thought, holy mackerel.

Did you know that 99% of men living in Warsaw prefer schnapps to vodka? Well, that's what the Poles say, anyway.

A cavalcade of limousines drove past my house today, escorting Barack Obama en route to Air Force One. I thought, trust me to mister President.

I was out cutting the grass when Red Indian women began falling from the sky. I thought, oh no, squawlly showers.

I call my dog Trebor. He's mint.

It wasn't easy writing a novel without punctuation. I had to pull out all the stops.

I went to make a donation at my local RSPCA centre yesterday and was shocked to see wallpaper hanging loose above a threadbare carpet. I thought, this place has gone to the dogs.

I took my children to a play area. I thought, oh no, not Twelfth Night again.

Cosmetic surgery's had its day...if you want my ex-pert opinion.

I stopped at a Jet garage and got stuck in a queue behind two RAF Tornados and a Singaporean Airlines Airbus A380.

Everyone in my village is highly intelligent and extremely sensible. We're living in fool poverty.

I opened the food cupboard and there was this tin of trembling soup, pleading for mercy. It was chicken.

I love my work in the kettle factory. In fact, I'm in my element.

There's an insect going round, dropping sweet wrappers and polystyrene chip trays. It's a right litter bug.

I was cooking an omelette when this streaker jumped in the mix and rolled round a bit before disappearing again. Not that I've seen him since. I think it was just a flash in the pan.

I've rented a flat above the hardware shop with my new girlfriend. We're living over the brushes.

That wicked witch near me is a real nasty piece of work. She's always flying off the broom handle.

I was driving along when I came across a sign saying, wig factory now closed. I thought, I'm on the road to no hair.

I stopped for a coffee and ended up buying a paperback entitled Planets and Galaxies of the Universe. I got it from Starbucks.

Sick of being ignored, I stuck twenty quid up the waiter's nostril then complained to the management. I said, I'm sick of coming here and having to pay through the nose.

I've got a new pen pal. His name is Bic.

I asked for a free quote. They sent me a dinner jacket.

My job at the savoury snacks factory: the pay is peanuts.

I went to bed with a tickly cough. I woke next morning with four legs, pointed ears and a thick mane of hair on the back of my neck. When the wife asked if I was feeling better, I said, not bad. I'm just a bit horse, that's all.

I saw this bloke in the pub, lambasting a glass of rum. Honestly, he was giving it a right old pep talk.

As a result of the worsening economic climate, I've finally fulfilled my lifetime's ambition and become an artist. I'm drawing the dole.

I stood for parliament but kept getting shouted down small, round cakes of flaky pastry. They were Eccles.

I raced my girlfriend to the camera shop. It was a photo finish.

They've started manufacturing beer in tablet form. Talk about a bitter pill to swallow.

The Beatles once played pontoon with a loud hailer. They even released a song about the experience: Twist and Shout.

I saw a coconut-filled, chocolate bar, walking down the street, wearing a gun and holster, and carrying rolled up wanted posters. I thought, ooh look, a bounty hunter.

So I said to this fruiterer, can I talk to you about bananas? He said, Fyffes? I said, if you think I'm paying for the privilege, you've another think coming!

I turned up for my dentists' appointment, covered in Red Indian war paint. I was trying to put a brave face on things.

Someone says there's a pig, hitch-hiking round the world in aid of charity? Talk about a globetrotter.

I hate my acupuncturist's job. I'd pack it all in tomorrow for two pins.

The bloke working the gaming table at the casino last night was celebrating his ninety-eighth birthday. He was an antique dealer.

I saw a sign on the motorway saying, Leeds 46 miles. I thought, that's a long way to go to a pet shop.

I've just had my engine tuned. Every time I switch on nowadays, I get blasted with Beethoven's sixth symphony.

My car broke down, so I called this number and was informed there was no call out charge. I said, that's no good to me. I need someone here in five minutes.

I left the pub early last night. There was a hen party on. It was all good fun, but I couldn't stand all that clucking.

I went to the pub and got poked in the eye by an antler. Flipping stag parties!

A mate of mine reckons he's an expert in Koi carp. I told him to get stuffed. Even I know fish aren't shy.

I bumped into the Black Eyed Peas yesterday. Apparently they'd had a right old fall out and decided to settle things in the ring.

How bad is the tele at Christmas? Mine spends all night at the pub then the next day throwing up.

I walked round this corner and there was the Mersey, Thames, Humber and Tyne, all performing a jitterbug. I thought, whey hey, river dance.

I'm writing a follow up to War and Peace, but think I may have bitten off more than I can chew. Honestly, it's like writing War and Peace.

I've just been fired. I'm a human cannonball.

Last time I went in Halfords, Kilimanjaro was in, buying a mountain bike.

I popped in a carpet shop and asked if they sold vinyl. When he said yes, I said, brilliant, do you have A Whiter Shade of Pale by Procul Harum?

Horses. They live for donkey's years.

I saw a gas meter slap an electric meter across the face with a glove. It was duel fuel.

I booked a free demo'. 8000 people turned up outside the Town Hall.

They're making a new film about classical European composers, with Arnold Schwarzenegger in the lead role. Asked which part he preferred, he said, I'll be Bach.

I've just had my dog micro-chipped. His name is McCain.

The motion detector on my CCTV is driving me mad. It goes off every time someone uses the bathroom.

I ordered a DVD from Amazon. When it arrived, I invited the delivery man inside for a nice cup of tea. I thought it only right after he'd crossed the Atlantic and paddled up a river 4000 miles long.

New tyres. They're highway rubbery.

I told the doctor that, when I feel tired, I get this irresistible urge to commit foul, heinous acts. He said, it sounds like you've got chronic fatigue sin-drome.

I think I'm turning into a shark. I'm going fin on top.

After a glittering career in domestic cleaning, that's it: I'm finally done and dusted.

I started work as an estate agent and immediately sold a bungalow that had been on the market for fifteen years. I thought, that should earn me a few house points.

Fingerless gloves. I can't see the point in them.

I had a TV dinner last night. The flat screen was lovely toasted, but the components were a bit on the tough side.

I made an exhibition of myself over the weekend. I went to the Tate Gallery, jumped on a plinth and stayed there for two whole days.

Prophets. They're living in the past.

I went in this shop and asked for a bottle of orange pop. The assistant said, small, medium or large? I said, you decide. Just try and Fanta size.

I tried manufacturing my own pork scratchings but the end result wasn't fantastic. If I'm entirely honest, I made a right pig's ear of it.

I saw a pack of wolves in Tesco. I thought, goodness gracious me: is there anything they don't sell?

A VG store married a Spar shop. It was a marriage of convenience.

I blew my savings on a new car for the girlfriend. Typical: I haven't heard a peep from her since.

Do you want to hear about my vegetable plot? It's the story of a spud that dumps a cabbage then elopes with a scabby carrot.

I've just been prosecuted for breaking into the marsupial house at London Zoo. Talk about a kangaroo court.

After months of soul-searching, I finally gave up my job as a ghost hunter.

I said, doctor, every time I take my shirt off, I shower the carpet with cobbles of coal. He said, that will be your arm pit.

I've just been whacked round the head by a copy of Oliver Twist. It hurts like the Dickens.

My stunning new girlfriend is a fantastic singer. She also has her own ceramics business. She's Bonnie Tyler.

I set up a market stall, selling moulded-metal military figurines. Everything sold except for the riderless steed. I thought, I'm flogging a lead horse here.

This highwayman held me up at gunpoint. He said, stand and deliver. I said, are you sure you want to go through with this? He said, a million per cent I am. In actual fact, I'm Adam Ant.

I was forced to give up my job at the bacon shop on medical grounds. It fetched me out in rashes.

She said, I've heard they've discovered an island inhabited solely by five-year-olds. I said, don't be so infant isle.

I've just been looking up at the moon. How on earth did a cow manage to jump over that?

I was drowning in quicksand when my mobile rang. He said, are you coming down the pub, or what? I said, I would, but I'm up to my neck in it at the moment.

The surprise party I arranged for my librarian girlfriend: the venue was double-booked.

I went on a booze cruise. The ship was full of wines and spirits, living it up on a trip round the Med.

I don't want to make it sound like I've an axe to grind...but a sharpening tool has gone missing from my garden shed.

I'm not saying my house needs a spring clean. But I've just seen a rat wearing overalls.

Earthquakes. They're not my fault.

I found a piece of map, blowing down the street. It was rip-off-Britain.

I sell replacement windows for use underwater. It's bubble glazing.

Did you hear about the fight between the llama and the ram? It was a right old ram a llama a ding dong.

I was watching this old film on VHS last night, a love affair set aboard an ocean-going liner on its maiden voyage. Half way through, it clobbered an iceberg and started taking on water. Then the tape snapped and I missed the end. I just wondered: did it sink?

Friar Tuck's descendant seems to be getting a lot of press coverage lately. Who is this Tummy Tuck, anyway?

I didn't last long at the stop smoking clinic. I was fed up with people blowing smoke up my backside.

My head was in a spin as the hangman slipped the noose round my neck. It's fair to say I was at the end of my tether.

Rolling roadblocks. If you see one coming, dive for cover.

I told my doctor I was having recurring dreams about unearthing the Ten Commandments. He said, go home and take these tablets.

I saw the college of performing arts, prancing down the street in a pair of ballet shoes. I thought, ooh look, a dancing school.

They say everyone's got a book in them. I know I have. I've just eaten Bravo Two Zero by Andy McNab.

I'm in the Guinness Book of Records. I've drunk more of the black stuff than anyone else in history.

I saw two shirtsleeves having an altercation. Nothing serious. Just a bit of fisti-cuffs.

My friend's a red coat. He spends all day on a hanger in Debenhams.

I arrived home with the wife to find the house swarming with insects. She opened her mouth to scream, but I clasped a hand across it before she had chance. I said, quiet, darling. I think we've been bugged...

I'm next in line for the throne. I would have been on it already if trap two hadn't been out of order.

I asked the way to the farm. This bloke said to look out for the A-road. He was right. I found this road, covered in hay, and there it was on the left.

I went to the doctors with a 100 watt bulb on my bonce. I was feeling a bit light headed.

My wife and I hate puzzles. We've never had a cross word in our lives.

I went to the video shop. I said, what do you think to The Karate Kid? He said, the carroty kid? You mean old Ginger behind the counter?

It started raining, and then there was this noise that sounded like applause. The wife said, what's that? I said, probably just a clap of thunder.

I ate a coat made from ice-cream. It was a Mac flurry.

I went to a cannibal's birthday party. We started off with a finger buffet.

She said, there's a dozen carol singers at the door, darling. I said, don't talk stupid, they're all boys.

I went to the barbers and had a number 2. I was made to clean it up then barred for life.

I've recently discovered I can bend it like Beckham. The doctor thinks I've got athlete's foot.

Herd of cows. Course I have. Where do you think we get beef from?

I went to the doctors for my annual MOT. I came out needing new brake pads and an oil change.

I was walking down the street when Red Indian braves began falling from the sky. The weather forecast was right for once: Apache outbreaks of rain.

The smell a fart leaves: it's for the benefit of deaf people.

I asked a spool of fishing line out on a date. It told me to get knotted.

I went to the surgery. I said, I've come for my prescription. The receptionist said, repeat? I said, I've come for my prescription.

Invalid butter toffee. It's not all it's cracked up to be.

There must be an election in the offing. I've just seen a politician buying a pair of canvass shoes.

I used to be a mean marine. I'm retired now but still tight.

My wife had a migraine. She said, bring painkillers, darling. Anadin. So I fetched her two paracetamol and turned the music up.

I could see dark clouds approaching, laced with drums and electric guitars. I thought, ooh look, here comes the band of rain we're expecting.

Graffiti. The writing's on the wall.

I said, doctor, I left the army six months ago but still feel like I'm on the parade ground. He said, don't worry. It's just hyper ten-shun.

Everyone says I'm stiff upper lipped. So what if I am? It's not my fault, is it, if my favourite drink is starch?

I was out snorkelling when I spotted six octopuses, forming a line and taking aim with rifles. I thought, ooh look, a firing squid.

I moved from Pyongyang to Seoul. I needed a change of Korea.

The wife's not happy with my new job. I've taken a pay cut to start work as a guillotine operative. Her parting words were, on your head be it...

I once fell out with a lumberjack. We were at loggerheads for weeks.

I heard silky smooth, blues vocals, coming from the bathroom. It was Lou Rawls.

I almost choked on a frog. I thought I was going to croak it.

Tennis. What a racket.

I've just seen a drunken au pair. Talk about nanny state.

It didn't get dark once for 365 days. It was a light year.

I went in the garage and was shocked to find that my new 2000cc car had eaten my electric drill, spanners and screwdriver set. It's my own fault. I should never have bought a tool eater in the first place.

I used to be a pilot in Biblical times. You may have heard of me. My first name is Pontius.

I'm not saying I'm old, but my first mobile was a carrier pigeon.

Everyone says my raincoat is a liar. I'm sick of all these Maccusations.

I said, doctor, I've bitten my tongue and I'm bleeding blue blood. Do you think I might be royalty? He said, take that ink cartridge out of your mouth and I'll have a look.

Sword fighting. I wouldn't mind a stab at it.

I was walking through the woods when I came across a group of shoes, plimsolls, wellies and trainers, putting up tents. I thought, whey hey, a boot camp.

My best friend at school was a cowboy. He was just like any other boy really. Apart from the big, furry head, of course, and an uncanny ability to yield milk.

I unearthed an unexploded World War Two bomb in my back garden. As I watched the army blow it up, I thought, that's a blast from the past.

When we go on holiday, my wife insists upon taking everything but the kitchen sink. This year, she even packed Encyclopaedia Britannica. That was when I finally put my foot down. I said, right, the book stops here.

I've made an absolute fortune from my online cosmetics business. Honestly, you couldn't make it up.

I love living in my house. It's right up my street.

Honeymoon? I thought it was made of green cheese?

I went to the doctors and there was this sign saying, examination in progress. The receptionist said it was blood tests.

Skydivers. They're so down to earth.

When I go on holiday, I prefer to arrive in resort at five in the morning. I'm a real fly by night.

I discovered a hedgehog in my pint. I thought, this has been spiked.

My sister Alison isn't without problems. Not only does she have an in-growing toe-nail, but bad breath as well. I've nicknamed her Ali-toe-sis.

I'm off to a sales meeting tomorrow. We're having it in the bored room.

I was in the pub when I heard ha-ha, bonk, and then saw this head go rolling across the floor. I was in on the joke as well but didn't think it was that funny.

I've just been sacked from my job in the R&D department at the crisp factory. Not that I'm surprised. I've never been what you'd call flavour of the month.

Pickaxes. They're ground-breaking.

I've just seen a winged insect, driving a Ford Transit and towing a caravan. I think it was a gypsy moth.

I thought I'd won the lottery, but it was all a big misunderstanding. This bloke rang me saying, Camelot, Camelot. But it was a wrong number. It was someone calling from Dubai, explaining his camel was hot.

I dropped the kids off at school and saw an infant revolver on its way into the classroom, carrying a lunchbox. It was the son of a gun.

I finished up getting Sky in the end. My roof blew off.

That brat off the Simpsons has been allowed to sneak into the country by some lorry driver called Edward, who is boasting the fact on the side of his trailer. You may have seen him: it's Eddie Stow Bart...

I've just seen the American football scores. Hawaii won five-0.

Two stinging insects, seeking overnight accommodation. First insect: The guest house opposite doesn't look bad. Second insect: Don't be stupid. It says B&B in the window. We're wasp and wasp.

I bought a home cinema system. Next thing, there was a long queue of people outside and a woman selling ice-cream in the hallway.

People with broken down cars. Tell them where to shove it.

I'm the bloke who paints zigzags around Pelican crossings. Not anymore, though. From now on, I'm going straight.

I rang this florists' shop. I said, your advert says telephone orders welcome? Do you mind if I put my Nokia Lumia 710 on? It wants to order flowers for its fiancé, a BlackBerry Curve 9360.

I said, what mobile phone network are you on? He said, O2. I said, oh really? Which two might that be, then?

I saw a big, pink footballer, with yellow spots, and strands of hair combed carefully across his scalp. It was Blobby Charlton.

It said on the back of this van, no stools left in this vehicle overnight. I said, don't you mean tools? He said, not really. I'm a pooh tester.

It's been announced that mutiny has broken out on a nuclear submarine. The navy have said the perpetrators are in deep water.

I opened the freezer and these squares of lattice potato were going on and on, and on, and all about nothing. I thought, oh no, potato waffles.

Charitable organisations. Something's got to give.

I was in a pub in Arbroath, watching racing from Kempton Park through the window. I couldn't believe it: the bloke sitting next to me thought it was on the tele.

I went to the doctors, complaining of double vision. Doctor Hourihane and Doctor Hourihane couldn't have been more understanding.

Newsflash: part time secretary accused of trying to kill her boss, Edward, has today been charged with a temp Ted murder.

I saw this bloke, using a long pole to ferry a young couple down the river in an upturned motor car. It was a Fiat Punto.

I went to the theatre and was surrounded by applauding Italian motor cars: Fiat Bravo.

I saw a Fiat, practising martial arts. It was kung fu Panda.

I've just seen Ebenezer Scrooge, running down the street with no clothes on. Talk about a mean streak.

I went into this perfume shop. I said, do you have anything by Dior? The assistant said, just a few baskets and a beep-beep anti-theft device.

Have you seen my flat mate? He's the one I was telling you about, the one who was run over by a steamroller.

I was on a cruise when the ship was boarded and robbed at gunpoint by bad copies of Rambo, Terminator and Toy Story. They were pirate DVD's.

I was a bit disappointed by my new 127 Hours DVD. The film was great, but I do think it should be renamed 94 minutes.

Daleks. They haven't got a leg to stand on.

I said, doctor, these spots on my skin won't stop singing, Deutschland, Deutschland, uber alles. He said, no wonder: they're German measles.

My daughter's doing really well in her exams, but tomorrow's chemistry. That will be the acid test.

I stopped for the barriers and a procession of chocolate coated confectionary passed in front of my car. It was a Revel crossing.

My wife spent a fortune on paper, pencils and crayons. Now we're overdrawn.

I saw a typist yesterday. It was hanging round my friend's neck, swigging on a bottle of gin.

There was water seeping from tins of soup in supermarket. When I checked the labels, it was just as I thought: potato and leak.

I saw a sign saying, pedestrians cross here. I couldn't comment, except to say that they didn't look too happy when I sped past at a hundred miles per hour.

There's an obese killer on the loose in the Arctic. It's the abdominal snowman.

I forgot to record the film, Knowing, starring Nicholas Cage. But never mind. It's not the end of the world, is it?

The little boy didn't eat his dinner money. It ate him.

I saw a sign saying, Saxon church. When I got there, it was a church alright, but covered in hessian mail bags.

The theft at the badge factory. Don't try and pin it on me.

Swans. They make me sick. All they do is swan around all day.

This surgeon stitched me up. Then he sold me a duff car.

It was nearly midnight when I arrived at the restaurant, and all they had left was puddings. Oh well, I suppose I got my just desserts.

So, what if my new girlfriend is made from lemon curd and pastry? Don't you go thinking she's a tart.

While my son was tidying his toy soldiers away, guess who was left holding the fort?

I've just held up Nat West with my magnum. I couldn't believe they were so petrified of vanilla ice-cream, coated in milk chocolate.

I've just had a sneak preview of next year's calendar. Take it from me, it's the future.

The insurance man called round and immediately made us switch the raunchy film off the tele. He was from the prude.

That brain transplant I was going to have. I've changed my mind.

It was crowded at the dead crow's funeral.

I was watching my next door neighbour doing his garden. First he dug it over, using a tool with a flat blade attached to a long handle. Then he had two cups of PG Tips. Talk about hoe tea-tea.

That woman with the stubbly chin has finally drunk herself to an early grave. She's the beer dead lady.

I can't stand my job at the knife factory. Too many backstabbers.

Dunroamin. It's a household name.

I went to the supermarket and was greeted by howls of laughter coming from the gravy aisle. I thought, whey hey, laughing stock.

I reckon there's been an acquisition error at the zoo. I popped round for a quick peek at the new gorilla, and it was dressed in combats, and brandishing hand grenades and an AK-47.

My three-year-old son has started work as a bodyguard. He's a child minder.

I bought one of those cross trainers but wish I hadn't. It's done nothing but shout at me.

My fitness instructor convinced me to try aerobics. Then I thought: hang on a minute, how are biros made from chocolate going to help me lose weight?

I've just had a hair transplant. Everything's fine now. I'm just a bit concerned about the buck teeth and big, floppy ears.

I went to the January sales. I bought January for £23.

Thieves broke into the National Railway Museum last night and stole the Flying Scotsman. Police are investigating multiple lines of enquiry.

I was strolling through the park, pondering why I owned the world's most disobedient dog. Then it came to me...

My son's a brilliant cricketer. He's also very lucky in raffles. Remember the name: Tom Bowler.

I'm taking over at the cake shop. It's a bun deal.

Novelists. They've lost the plot.

So I said to this literary agent, I've got a fantastic book idea. He said, put it in writing.

Gingers Rogers and Fred Astaire. They were good. But I wouldn't make a song and dance about them.

I bought two new friends yesterday. I went to Pal Mall.

That big silver thing on my drive, between you, me and the gatepost, it's my car...

I was on the sands with Martha. She was eating muffins. I said, save one for me, one for me, one for me. It was echo beach.

I went in a craft shop. I said, how much for commercial towing vehicle Nostromo?

My interview at the men's underwear factory went really well. The boss said I ticked all the boxers.

I was offered a job in a teddy bear factory. I told them to get stuffed.

I was offered a job in a turkey factory next. I told them to get stuffed as well.

As I was being wheeled to theatre, I spotted a thirty foot oak, wearing green scrubs and face mask, approaching from the opposite direction. The nurse said not to worry. It was just a tree surgeon.

I said, doctor, I keep my iPhone on my bedside table and it's keeping me awake at night. He said, you've got sleep App near.

I was arrested for stealing a hamburger from McDonalds. The police gave me a right grilling.

My bookcase is huge. Multi-story, in fact.

I'm putting money aside for a rainy day. I'm saving up for a new brolly.

I used to be a turf accountant. I filled out tax returns for wealthy lawns and football pitches.

The scandal at the toothpaste factory: it's Colgate.

I saw a big factory picking on a small factory. I thought, that's workplace bullying.

The new bloke at work, the one with too much skin for his head, he's finally resigned. I can't say I'm surprised. It was obvious from day one his face didn't fit.

I'm attempting to make the Guinness Book of Records for the longest time spent indoors without using nail clippers. I'm in growing toe nail.

If you're tempted to buy that book, 10 Minute Meals, don't bother. Minute? They were absolutely minuscule.

I'm feeling a bit down in the mouth. I've just eaten a duck.

I've put my laptop into hibernation mode. It's in a cardboard box under the stairs, wrapped in old newspapers and straw.

The bloke who invented denim: pure jeanius.

I clocked one of my old friends yesterday. I hit him over the head with a digital alarm.

My friend Macy has opened a chemist shop. I reckon he'll go phar.

I've just received an MMS from a bloke in Houston. It was a Tex message.

Doctor Who landed a job as a health and safety officer with Osaka borough council. On his first day, he went back to 1944 and immediately grounded 122 Kamikaze pilots for not wearing helmets.

William Hartnell, Patrick Troughton, Jon Pertwee, Tom Baker, Peter Davison, Colin Baker, Sylvester McCoy, Paul McGann, Christopher Eccleston, David Tennant and Matt Smith. Who do they think they are?

I was out horse riding when I spotted a group of women in wedding dresses coming from the opposite direction. I was on a bridal path.

There was this sign on the motorway, which said, Barnsley 9 Sheffield 26. I thought, blimey, that must have been some match.

I used to be a public relations officer at the bicycle factory. I was the spokes person.

I never turned up for my interview at the dairy. I bottled it.

An articulated lorry has spilled its load of office supplies across three lanes of the M1. Traffic in the area is described as stationery.

I couldn't believe it when I spotted a sign in the cafe saying, today's special. I've still not found out who told them it was my birthday.

My friend keeps livestock in the kitchen. He has a plough in his dining room and bales of straw in the hall. He lives in a farm house.

I've just resigned from my job at the pottery. It was a right mugs game.

I bought the Daily Mirror. I couldn't believe it: there was a picture of me on the front page.

Unwrapping my Christmas presents, I discovered a severed head. The next parcel contained a torso, and the one after that an arm and a leg. Casting a glance at the pile of unopened boxes, I thought, hmmm, something's definitely afoot...

Stephen King stopped me the other day and asked if I knew the way to Sheffield city allotments. I thought, he's lost the plot.

I went in this pub, and there was this woman, balancing a pint glass on her head, playing snooker. Someone said it was Beatrix. I said, Beatrix who? He said, beer tricks potter.

I could tell you a joke about a brick wall. But you'd never get over it.

As I spoon-fed my one-year-old son, he began to lecture me upon the nutritional value of mass produced baby feeds. I thought, hark at him in his high chair.

It said on the back of this van: Mob: 07741 897103. So I rang the number. Ten minutes later, I had the Sicilian Mafia camped out on my doorstep.

Printed in Great Britain
by Amazon

184R00069